SPOKEN WORD

selected poems: 2003-2013

Copyright 2013 by Marcus Amaker.

No part of this publication may be reproduced, stored in a retrieval system, or transmitted in any form or by any means electronic, mechanical, photocopying, recording or otherwise without the prior permission of the publisher.
ISBN-13: 978-1537669762
ISBN-10: 1537669761

LOVE IS AS NEAR AS YOUR NEXT BREATH

14 sabbath
15 shelter
16 queen
18 firmaments
19 faith
20 dry land
22 ten years
23 in this light
24 depth of field
30 the youth decay
32 upper king
34 for/ever
35 the soft paper cut
36 pathways
38 the pulse
40 heartline/bloodline
42 dear delilah
44 at the dawning
46 open
48 jazz
56 making love with only words
58 time
60 rosemary
61 prayer
62 rescue me from me
63 sapphire
64 her zephyr

66 cracks in the marrow
68 the mirror
69 foundation/shaken
70 we could (be)
71 the perception of sound
80 something fragile
82 until the september equinox ...
84 with luna ...
85 dear someone
86 what i knew of love
87 unlearning the ego of the earth
88 incandescence.
89 the light belongs to you
90 the girl and our gallery
91 my hand, on her heart
92 the present presence
94 dialogue with our ghosts
96 what is of our experience
106 your arrival (an open letter)
108 ... and she is still dancing
110 the symphony of streetlights
111 dewdrops
112 golden
114 giving birth
116 on the surface
      and underneath
118 holding your breath

120 on meeting/death
122 it's the ghosts
123 a resistance
124 the fifth
126 alarm clock (flashing red)
127 unwinding
138 while looking up
139 the tapdancer
140 on conversation
142 after taste
144 dry
146 the fabric of us
148 charlotte and i
149 brushstrokes
150 a life in layers
152 a study in stasis
154 birthmarks
156 (the blood that runs)
158 we speak the same language
160 vertebrae
170 under our dream's illusion
172 there are so many things we can not see
174 stir the embers
175 learning to live wicked
176 heartbeat songs
178 the cloudbuster
180 wayfaring
182 in the gloaming
183 au fait
184 awakened (part 2)
186 we are, lifelines
188 mantra
189 star
194 love
196 side effecting
198 carolina
200 the dance
202 82 days
204 spark
205 patchwork
206 rites of passage
208 terrorism
210 sunspots
212 purple heart
214 the summer of our first memory
215 the overflow

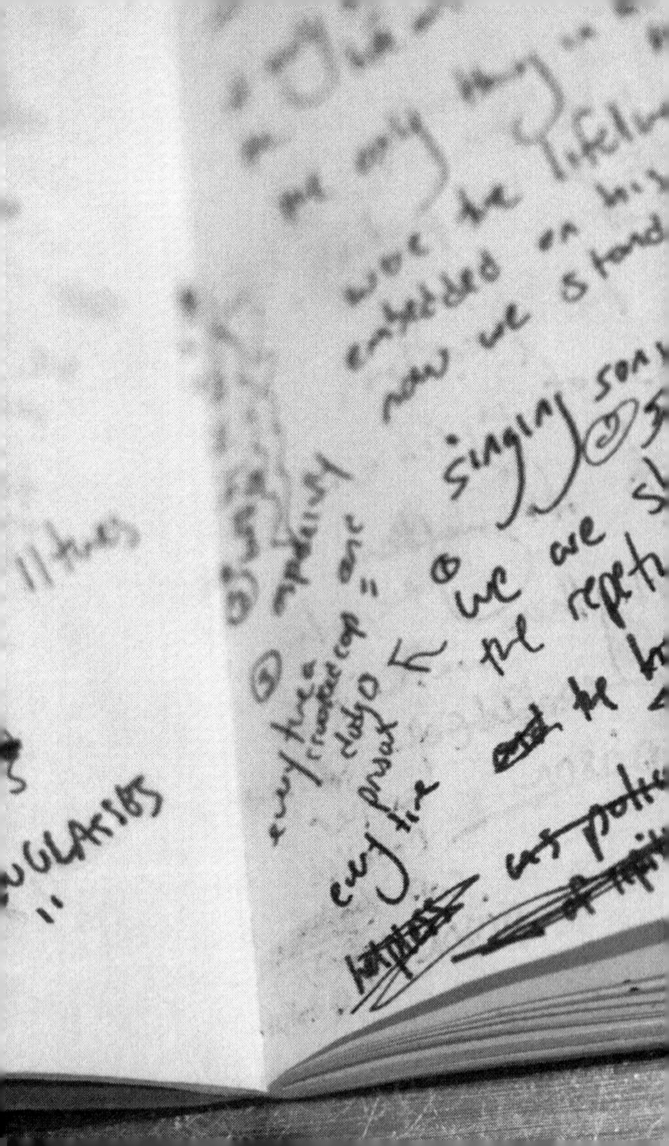

panthers,
injustice.
as rhythm,
is like the prison
as written in
four bars
doing prison bars
cotton fields.
jail to nowy on 26 y/o world

sabbath

on sundays, we are most aware
of our need for awareness.
the mornings fall into our laps
like asheville snow
and time melts away quickly
like youth disappearing from a baby
born into melancholy.

on sundays, we let the stillness win
after going into war
with saturday night's movement.
our armor lays silent by the bed
under a blanket of smoke,
and our clothes reek of
memory's aftermath.

on sundays, work gets done
by not working at all.
we speak with silent words,
comfortably in the nest of
each other's arms.

shelter

there are mirrors here,
but the reflections
don't look him in the eye.
he is a stranger in his own home.
the neighbors walk
through the living room
like mimes,
actors in a rushed production,
tongue-tied with silence.

he sets the roof on fire
and flushes the smoke down the sink
with soot-soaked fingers.
he's constantly sweeping conversations
under the rug to make room for
dusty handshakes
and clean getaways.

there are mirrors here, but
the reflections are blurred,
caught up in their own vanity,
unwilling to pay the rent.

queen

i thought i knew what love looked like
when it stood before me
as royalty, devoid of diamonds
and emotion, robbed of its wealth.

i thought i knew what love felt like
as i walked up to its majesty's court,
and ran my fingers against crowns on
dusty statues.

i saw signs of love's treasure
in distant kingdoms,
across roads i couldn't reach
with endless maps
casting silent shadows
on tired feet.

but i never knew what love sounded like
until it was whispered in my ear
by a voice whose inflection
was a reflection of our rapture.
whose birdsong
was the calm of our mornings
spent holding each other
in holy moments,

because love is as near as your next breath
with its arms outstretched.
and its richness,
finally revealed.

firmaments

If the sky were made of mirrors,
some people would project their image
over the airwaves
as if their light had nothing to do
with the sun
laying just beyond their reflection.

If the sky were broken glass,
some people would throw stones
at the fragments
of their own shadow.

If we were in heaven,
someone would find a reason
to stare at their feet,
walking blindly on sacred ground,
tripping on their own tragedy.

faith

because I am ready for love,
I walk toward the present without
a receipt of the past in my pocket,
freeing myself from the future fantasy that
unfolds in my mind.

because I am ready for love,
my canvas contains more than just
variations of black and white
because life
is more than just black and white
opposing itself in colorful conflict.

because I am ready for love,
your hands feel familiar
as if we were never strangers,
fumbling through forced first impressions.

because I am ready for love,
there is no burden in death
or belief in the separation of solitude
because we will be connected forever.

dry land

dancing in between the raindrops
and dodging self doubt
on a downhill slope.
dreaming of one-way streets
where memories
are held for safe keeping,
but digging in the dirt
for the key to a
different path.

what will he ask of God?
will it be the slow beat of
his heart beating,
breaking the silence of depression?

will it be the dream
of a dormant chorus -
drowning out the dirge
of his inner demons?

no.
today, he asks God for
a little dry land,
for the sting of
humidity to not touch his skin.

for the salt of the earth
to not singe open wounds,
for the wind to guide him safely home
despite the roadblocks of his brain
and the floods that never
seem to drain.

ten years

i wonder what would happen
if you walked in on me at a bar,
having conversations
with a dimly lit corner
instead of the flashing neon lights
running on pure energy,
staring at the night ahead with
flashes of uncertainty.
most likely, you'd sit with me
and offer a drink,
then tell the bartender to pour
strong words of encouragement
into the glass.
after a brief moment,
i'd write your story on a napkin,
and give it to you in the form of a poem.
you'd probably read it ten years later,
sitting at a bar by yourself,
remembering when the ice cubes
blurred into each other
like a watered down dream.

in this light

in this light, even the sun
seems inadequate. just when
i adjust to your open air,
a luminous moment comes
to us, and the future is undimmed,
unobstructed by the dark. forever,
in this house, is where we uncover
the truth. our love now
shares a space with the kitchen sink,
the stares, the bed. unafraid of silence,
we alter fear into fearlessness,
building flames and frames
for memories yet to come.
unashamed.

depth of field

memories fade like dreams
that slip away in waking moments.
each scene plays like a movie -

you wrote the script
and the actors are strangers,
reciting lines in a foreign language,
learning the ways of the world
through a foggy camera lens.

your mind is trapped
in the present
but your eyes shift forward,
focusing on the future
and forgetting the past.

where do the memories go?
are they packed in the closet
of your mind, collecting dust
next to age-old mistakes
like pants that no longer fit,
shoes that have gone out of style,
gifts that have lost their meaning?

where do the memories go?
do they tire of you
using them for your own enjoyment,
like old toys, living in boxes,
waiting to be donated to
the next playwright?

you watch yourself on screen
and wonder –
who did the makeup?
who picked the clothes?
and who chose the cast?

photo by jordan freeman

the youth decay

remember the honey-dipped sound of sin, stretched out through smoke-drenched sorrow, where strangers danced to the backbeat of 80s music tickling their hips. remember how i burned with fire as my hands stayed curved along the icy cold slopes of slippery cocktails. remember the sound of alarm clocks and grown children scrambling for their mothers, masked in youth and perfumed skin. remember how you looked at me to see yourself because all of the mirrors were broken and you saw how beautiful you were. remember the moment you turned your back and i whispered "lust" because i knew you wouldn't hear. remember the empty conversations that echoed through the scandals taking place in the room next door, down the street, and on cell phones. remember life as a perfect narrative succumbing to imperfection once the lines begin to blur. remember the wet sound of truth quenching the thirst of dried-up lovers before eventually bathing in little white lies. i will remember my fingernails on strangers leaving marks on the decay of the night.

upper king

i see poems everywhere
in my neighborhood.
they write themselves -
stumbling through winter's relentless stare
and blinded by the bluntness of spring.

they surround you
before you slip
into the sweet darkness
of a sour night,
sorting through a history
of scrambled words.

i am the tongue-tied baby of the family.
the wide-eyed wanderer
who finally found a home.
walking past the broken down buildings
that hold the streets together
and having real conversations with america -
admiring her ball gowns
down one-way streets
while washing off the doom
of her repugnant perfume.

i see poems everywhere in my neighborhood.
they are the graffiti artists of the sky,
the glowing conversations
written in the stars,
the phone numbers
typed into cell phones,
the endless puddles of alcohol
that linger like rain in an unholy city,
looking for God amongst the ghosts within.

for/ever

they emerge
from the fountain of youth
wringing out their clothes
from the highs and lows
of liquid daydreams,
not wanting
to get their feet wet
in dirty water
or look for the promise
of another
endless,
mundane
waterfall.

they emerge
with wrinkled skin
and salty tongues
looking down
at their reflection
and seeing
two sets of eyes
now
one.

the soft paper cut

if you were a book of poems,
i'd wake up every morning
with ink on my fingertips
and the smell of fresh paper
etched in my mind.

i'd carry you with me
for morning coffee
and run my hands
up and down your spine
before absorbing
the breadth of your pages
and exploring
your body of work.

you'd accompany me
sitting under an oak tree
and we'd lose ourselves in each other,
line by line
until i have every inch of you
memorized.

if you were a book of poems
i'd take you to bed
and you'd be the last thing i'd see
before falling asleep.

pathways

you've been down this road before.
lacing up your solitude
and tightening down your shoelaces
for the ride.
and suddenly
you remember what it feels like to fly
after crawling around your house
for days at a time.

shaking off the gray is clarity
and you gracefully flow
in and out of color.
your hands are weary from
coloring outside of the lines
and ink bleeding through
the pages of your life.

then wind smacks you in the face
and you are awake. wide awake,
no longer laying down for your dreams.
it seems
perfect.

there are pathways for your heart
to beat faster and faster.
roads opening up to lead you somewhere,
anywhere from the echoes of your home.

the air is sweeter now.
it flirts with you like a woman,
winking at you through the breeze
and you pass by trees
like years of your life,
swaying back and forth
for so many years,
you've lost count.

let go of your fears
and you'll lose your balance.
it beckons you to keep holding on
with one hand, at least
to stay on the path
from a sidewalk
to the open road.

the pulse

charleston,
where the sidewalks scream on saturday nights
and the corners rotate budding musicians
with skin-tight dreams.
where strings of pearls search for salvation
then sweat out their frustrations
on the backs of rooftops.
where the homeless sprout
like weeds through concrete
seeking two dollars, a handshake
and a little bit of sunshine.
where the humidity chokes you out of breath
but you manage to speak to the
spit-shine waiters who serve 95 dollar
bottles of wine.
where two blocks away,
a five dollar pitcher of liquid gold
spills on the canvas of sticky floors.

charleston,
where love lingers on cobblestone streets
in narrow alleyways, and the smell of sex
is the foundation for first and last impressions.
where shadows are surrounded by the ocean
and sea-seeing people gasp for air

from knee-deep bills and dirt-cheap thrills.
where those with
no sense of history's melody
will sync with the songs of the city's slaves.
where the poets scrape stanzas
off of streetlights
and if they scream loud enough, maybe
someone will hear

because we are all the same,
we are all the
same.
we are all
the same

heartline/bloodline

my grandmother's hands
show age
like
her heart
shows beauty.

her voice,
deep and feminine,
wraps around words
as slow as
the sweat that
finds its way down
our forehead on this day,

when she and i
walked together,
arm in arm,
over humid
tombstones
deep into the memory
of mother earth.

sometimes
i feel like
we are strangers
and sometimes
we are mirrors
of
each other.

dear delilah,

i want you to believe
i am as strong as samson
every time you lay with me
and unlock the thoughts
that are hidden
beneath layers of tightly woven locs.

i want you to think of me as a lion,
calmly walking through
a forest fire of mystery -
the king of his domain,
the ruler of ash.

i want to be strong enough
for you to ride on my back
and latch on to the muscles
that arch and bend to your body
when we make love.

but delilah,
it's moments like these
when i gain my strength from you
and the way your hair
looks in the morning,

tangled in my mane,
as you sleep.

it's you
who finds me in the wild
and brings me back home
when i am weak.

at the dawning ...

how do you stand still
when God is an earthquake,
shaking the ground
beneath your feet?

how do you act cool
when love is a volcano,
erupting fire in your veins?

how do you tiptoe
around the remains of the past
that lay sleeping
in the darkened corners of your mind?

how did you find
yourself drowning in desire
after your heart
suffered a deep drought?

why do we doubt love
when its truth is never hiding,
and why does it remind me
of the red sun's rising?

what are the questions
we are afraid of,
and how do i get
to the answers?

open

even though i never
gave you the key,
you unlocked me.
and now i am open
to endless possibility
and we will no longer
close doors
or shut windows
because the light
is too bright to deny,
and the wind,
whispering kisses
into the room,
will listen as my fingers
unlock the mysteries
of your body.

i am open for you
like the road that will guide you
coast to coast
and hold you in its arms.
you are a newborn baby
looking up at the sky,
wide-eyed and open,

waiting for life's
infinite, woven tapestry
to wrap your soul
in its wonder
and unfold miles and miles
of new memories.

i understand
you need to be lost,
because your roadmap
opened you up to me
and you are not free
to take our journey.
but we'll both look up
when you grow wings
and i'll tilt my head west
and catch feathers
on my tongue,
and you'll stare at the sun,
feel my warmth,
and know exactly where to find me.

jazz

the morning rises with smoke
and the water drowns out the sky,
washing your music away.

new orleans,
you were silent today.

your muted colors
were splashed upon television screens,
your ink
darkened newspapers,
smearing silhouettes all over our hands
and we are helpless and
restless with worry -
wondering when Bourbon St. will dance
again,
when men will make love to the evening
air
with saxophones,
where someone soaks up the atmosphere
with spicy cajun food,
speaking creole.

new orleans,
you have so much soul.

and now i dream in jazz rhythms,
closing my eyes to feel the drumbeat
that rests steady beneath the ruin

it echoes -
heavy, with the heartbeat of families
forced to flee the floodwaters
where melodies no longer float through the air,
instead they lay there,
unable to breathe.

but you will find your beat again.
it will rise with the morning air
and the water will sing to the sky
and our tears will write new songs
for jazz to sing.

STARE AT THE SUN, FEEL MY WARMTH,

AND KNOW EXACTLY WHERE TO FIND ME

- expose — + boundaries, to what
- perception of ___

- work + no ___
  presence
- september
  equinox
- uppsala
- system ___

road

- getaway + rhyme, girl ___
  chartotte ?
- cloudbust
  — jaza
- present
  Clar___

social network
Spotify

- pressure Janici
- appu king   coldjet
- cloudbuster
- at the door) + m/h had
   your) your arrival) girl gallery /berent,
- charlotte   inspect
- carolina   tissue
   shre
   (my birth) & what's
   develops uncovers of
                    spaces

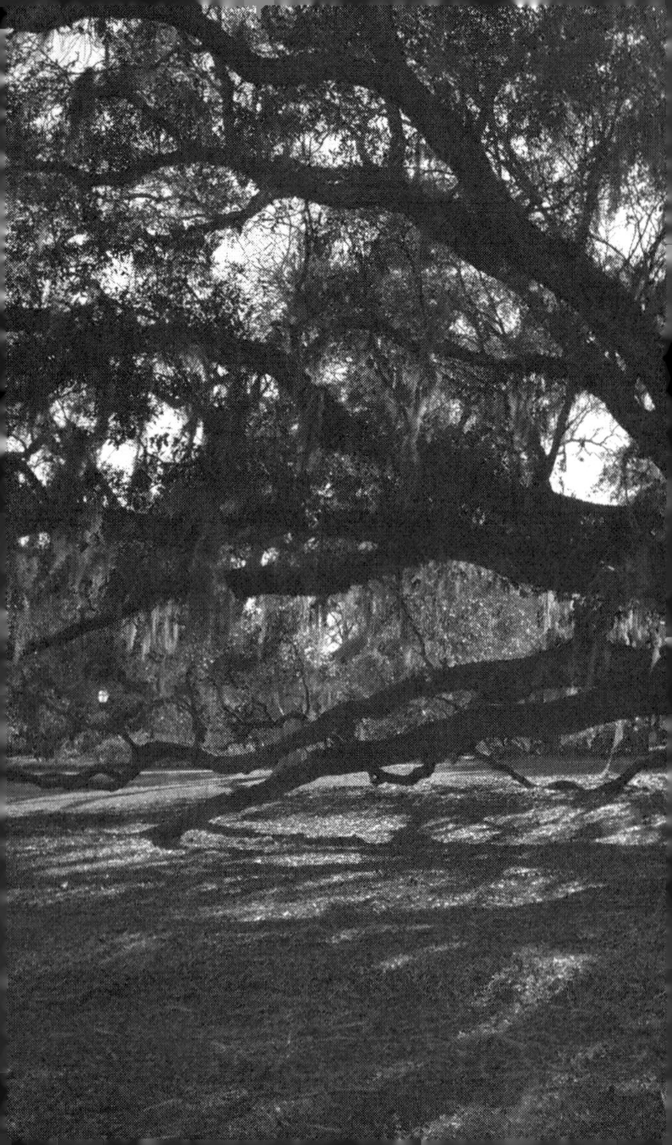

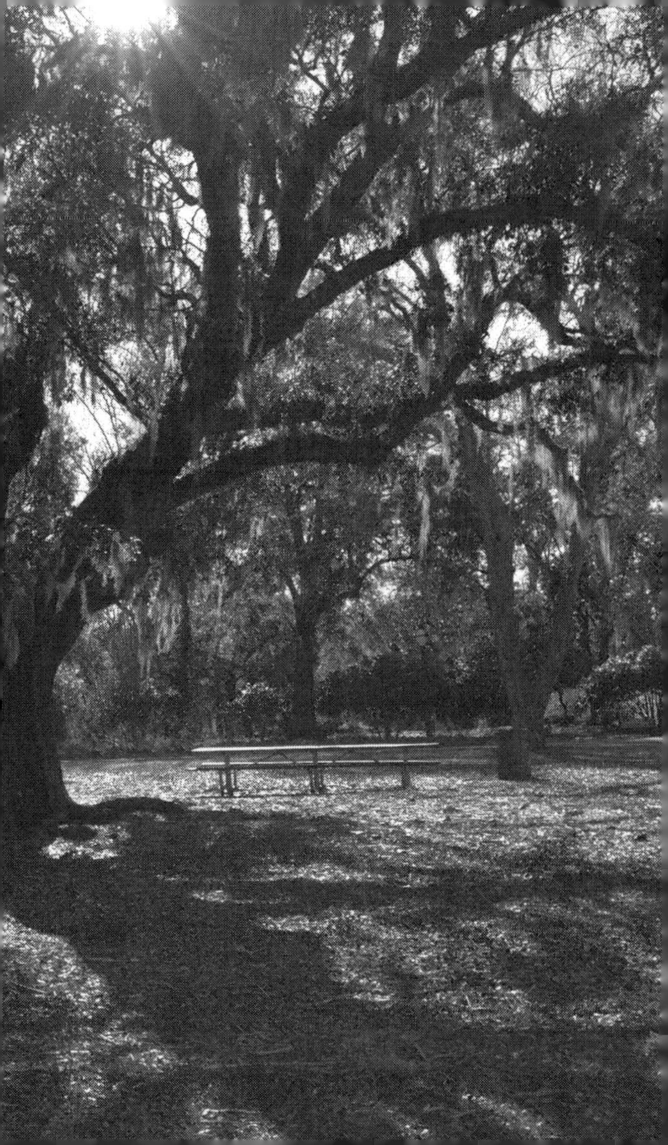

making love with only words

i like how we are
heavy, without
tipping the scale.
beautiful, without
makeup and mirrors.
dancing, without
listening to music.
wanting, without
needing.

i like how we
don't need poems
to be poetic.
how you say so much
without speaking.
by just breathing
next to me.

i like how we
learn so much
without knowing.
by just glowing
in the bright spots.

my eyes are closed
and i can
see you.

time

let me know
if it's tomorrow
we're supposed
to look forward to.
because

she is probably
looking forward to
yesterday
before all of her
tomorrows decided
to unravel.
in a split

second, we, too,
will one day
wake up and wish
it was yesterday.
until then,

we will waste
the time
we were given

as someone clings to the
time
they have
left.

rosemary

my feet roam scorched earth, kicking up
the dust of fine-toothed footprints,
covered in ash. the skeletons of skin
are bathing in sin,
blowing embers through lungs and
running around like dogs in heat.
in the sea of a thousand dying flames,
 you never lost your spark. the memories,
thick as smoke, rose with wings
from our fire. and i sit, burning
through blank sheets of paper, peeling
back layers and welcoming the scars.

prayer

let me stand with grace
on unstable ground,
lean toward the light
that i came from,
the same light
i will leave with.

let me sleep soundly
when wolves are wide awake,
walk when my mind
is running off course,
jump in the water
of my deepest fear
and come away
with my courage
swimming in the strength
of a thousand oceans.

let me live
when death surrounds me,
sing when my lungs
are out of breath,
look to the heavens
when the earth
weighs me down.

rescue me from me

rescue me from awareness
when i am sleeping in your garden.

loosen the grip of nightmares
haunting my daydreams.

walk me along a path of fire
when my heart has been burned.

hold my hand
when i am clutching indecision.

call me by my truth
before you call me by my name.

wish upon me brightly
like you wish upon the stars.

look at me
the way you looked at love
before you labeled anger.

rescue me from drowning
when language leaves me dry.

sapphire

you put diamonds in my pockets
every time you disappear,
and i carry you around
the mining of my mind
after seeing what lies
beneath your surface.

we'll always
dig for the gold that sleeps under our feet
because nothing is as beautiful
as the treasures of the earth
and the light it takes
to uncover the mystery.

when silver lines your hair,
i'll gladly bear the mark
of diamond dust
and nickel-plated memories
to fumble through dusty pockets
and find you.

her zephyr

do you want the wind to play with?
if so,
which way would the trees sway?
would they uproot
from where they were planted
and fall somewhere
closer
or carry you gracefully
closer
to me?

i'm curious.

i'm curious when windows
rattle me from sleep
and gravity
releases its grip on the ground.
i'm curious
when something sweet
is in the air
and wherever i go, it's
there.

do you want the wind to play with?
if so,
would it unfold your wings
and guide you to me,
willingly?

i'm curious.

cracks in the marrow

i saw my reflection on TV,
buried beneath the rubble.
the landscape of my face
drowning with grief
as tears shook the foundation of my heart
like an earthquake.

there are cracks in the marrow
of mother earth.
her heart hides mass graves of burden,
piled high beneath invisible pain.

and now we know what it looks like -
it's the faces of men forever masked in
sorrow, and a mother walking slowly into
tomorrow.

building hope on the back
of a swollen landscape
that's spinning with chaos.

dear haiti,
today i feel like we are one
i am nothing more than your lost son

searching for his brothers among the
spirits spiraling down,
looking for the sky for solid ground.

dear haiti,
the promise of your survival
shines like starlight, rising in the winter sky.
in spite of gravity, you will fly.

the mirror

i took a picture of you the day before
the world ended, and your smile
was as bright as a memory. your
hair fell over your face like man's
fall from grace, and we dissected time
with a fine-toothed comb. "we are
going to die tomorrow," i thought.
and you said, "all we have is now."
now, the earth passes through
faded photographs - snapshots of
the sun rising over restless rooftops.
clocks ticking for prisoners of gravity,
rain dripping from the sky like chipped
paint. umbrellas unfurling into fear.
now, the photo hangs in a frame. a
frozen moment of clarity in the warm
comfort of confusion. i remember you
telling me "there is no afterlife because
there is no death." then, i didn't believe
you because i was in the dark room
of my mind, processing pictures of
what i wanted the world to look like
instead of stopping to see it through
the right kind of light.

foundation/shaken

an invisible force
moves through the room,
even for those
who are unaware of its presence.

like tree branches shaken by the wind,
desire is a movement.

but i am fearful
of a real revolution
and how emotions
loot my heart.

but i am open.
ultimately,
always open
for the change.

we could (be)

what if I
saw the sun in your eyes
and it was
a reflection of me?

what if we
were endless words
bound together
by the book of love,
flipping through chapters
like age -
each page
a note
in our collective symphony?

what if we
could give each other
the beginning of memory
with the chords written in our skin
like instruments of a familiar song?

what if God
felt like
you feel?
would it be real?
could this be,
love?

the perception of sound

just when you think your heart only beats for the dark, a light overtakes silence and a jazz band steps on stage. the music swirls around your glass, each note gets under your blood and you are dizzy with love. you've heard this song before, but not like this. it's like the singer knows your kiss and each note is impossible to miss. don't hold your applause, this might last forever. instead, pause and enjoy the encore that's happening at this very moment. it taps you on the shoulder after you've danced with complacency, and suddenly, you are face to face with the woman who placed an echo into soundproof walls; who has never played an instrument like this before. just when you think your heart only beats for the dark, you find yourself light-headed, obsessed with the wonders of her music and waiting for the miracle to happen.

THE MUSIC SWIRLS AROUND YOUR GLASS, EACH NOTE

GETS UNDER YOUR BLOOD AND YOU ARE DIZZY WITH LOVE

photo by jordan freeman

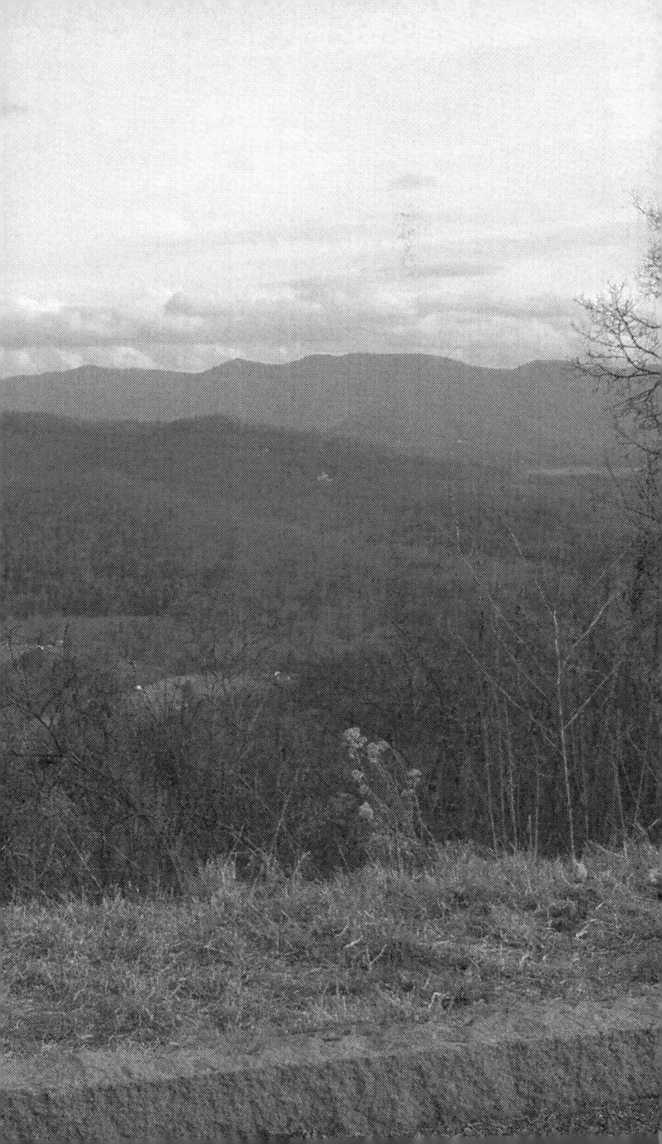

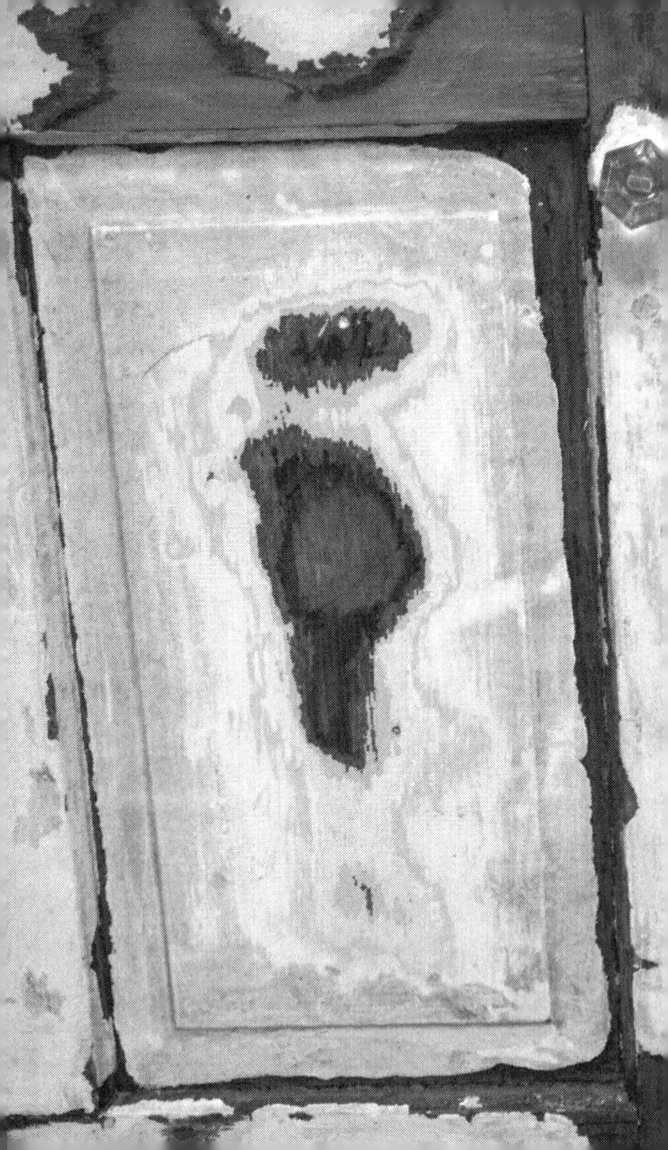

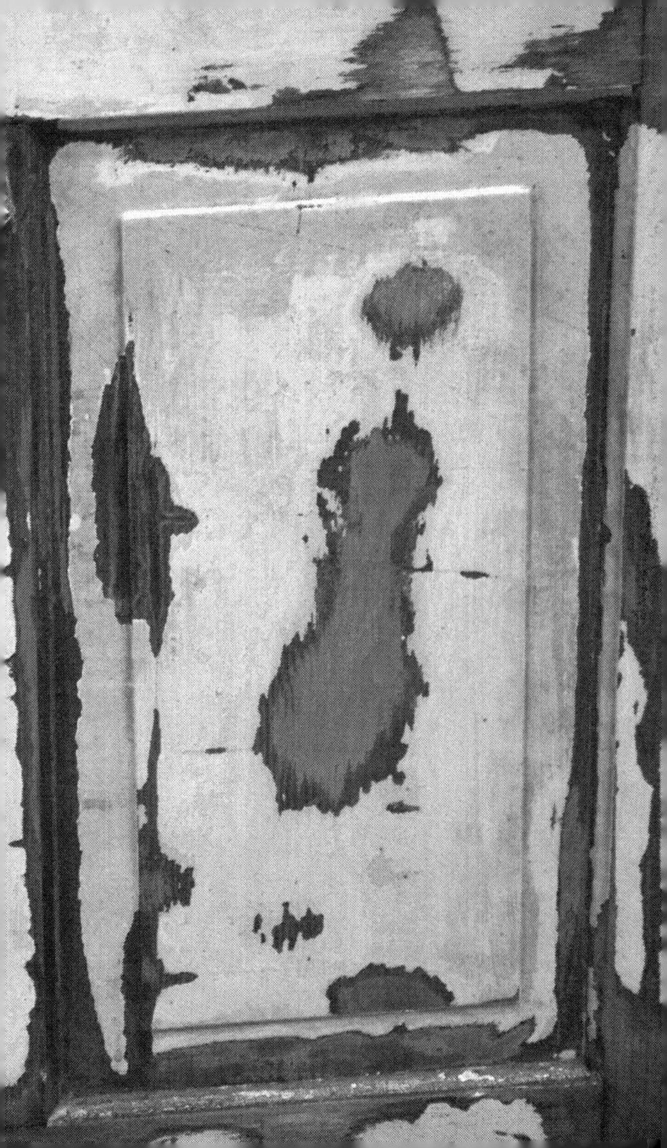

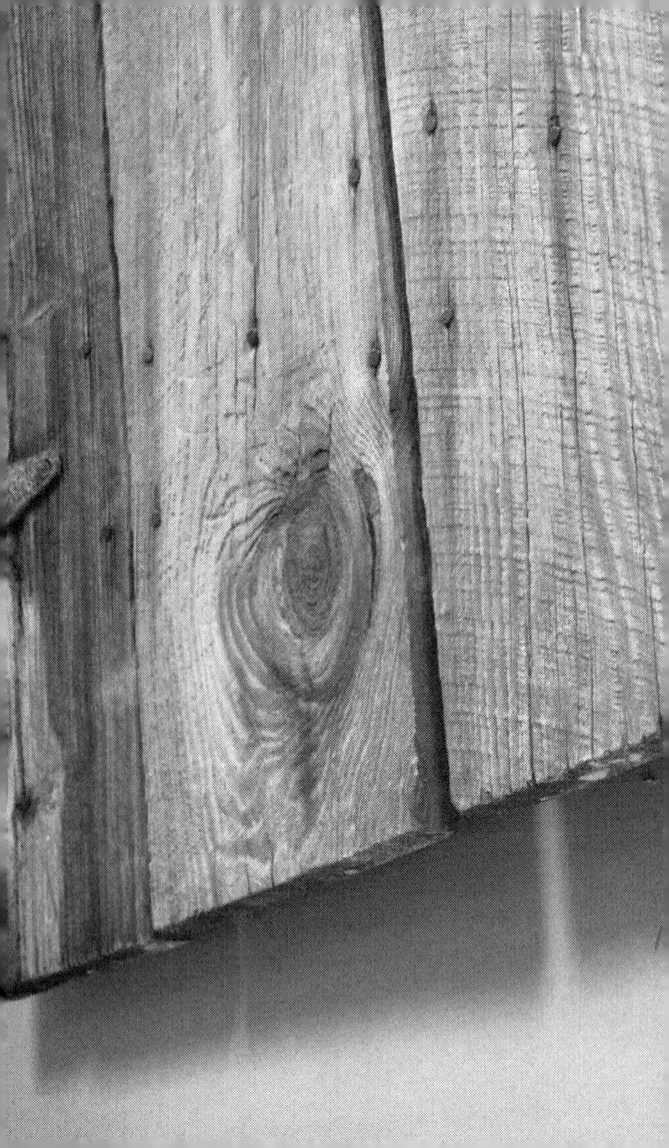

something fragile

i've spent most of my life
trying to find peace
when broken pieces of the earth
unfold in front of me.
when the holes in my shoes
are the blisters of my heart,
searching for patches
of perfect pavement.

but i keep finding pieces of love
scattered across the ground like glass
as tourists pass in speeding cars,
splashing each poem that shuffles by.

in Charleston,
pieces of history clutter the streets.
and love is a hurricane
that tore down my walls long ago.
each violent wind
breaks off a piece
of my soul,

so i am left
trying to find peace
among the shards of sexuality,
the fragments of foolishness,
the aftermath of affection.

until the september equinox ...

in the winter,
i will watch you from afar
and fall to bed
wrapped in the warm, woven folds
of anticipation
then wake up and wash off
the crimson that kissed me
into colorful dreams.

in the spring,
i am awake and in bloom,
a beacon for your light.
a bird in flight,
floating along
the winds of change.

in the summer,
we are careful yet careless,
burning deep fires of mystery,
sweating from the proximity
and scared to burst
into flames.

in the fall,
you are the queen before the sea
and the branches of doubt
that fall away from me
in the quiet, cool air,
that whispered the birth
of our love,
of our love ...

with luna

tonight, the moon is a woman
and she is our escape.
her silver shadow hangs thick
over a horizon of sleepy stars
and her eyes make bold advances
toward the sun.

you are her favorite daughter -
a lunar eclipse among stargazers,
unaffected by the sky's flirtation with
dawn.

i am nothing more than earthshine -
orbiting into daydreams,
silently reflecting her light.

dear someone

make sure you don't
shine too bright,
because i just might
plant myself in this desire,
lean toward the longing
and warm myself to you,
forever.

what i knew of love

i painted a picture of you
with my eyes closed.
the lines on your face
were replaced
by an angel's imperfections.

each brush stroke
was an empty reflection -
a vacant remembrance
of what it was like
to worship you;
to not completely
see you.

my house is a museum
of rusted frames -
bound together
by moments of blind faith,
portraits of
past mistakes.

i painted a picture of you
during a dream
and sleepwalked
under the light
of our honeymoon.

unlearning the ego of the earth

my body
is a stranger
to my soul -
parts of me
have become
separated,
stretched across
a planet
of indecision.

the body of water
under my skin
is fighting against
the tides of my mind,
drowning in fear.

and i have
poured poison
in the ocean,
erected buildings
on bones,
planted seeds
on concrete
and paved
a crooked road
to heaven.

incandescence.

i've looked down on myself
in rooms with glass ceilings
as thoughts came crashing down
on the hardwood floors
inside a mansion of expectation.

and i tiptoed around the living room,
walking on broken pieces of light
swept under the rug.

this morning,
the light broke through my mind's shadow
and it looked like God -
blanketing the bedroom like a ghost,

an unseen force
piecing together
the path of my past.

the light belongs to you

you were the flame
before the phoenix,
born on the fourth of July,
the boy who poured his heart
into the sky.

on the day you died,
i tiptoed calmly
through the forest of your memory
then walked into
the rising stillness of reality,
the absence of your smile.

tonight, i can not think of you
without locking fingers with trees,
clinging to a life beyond breathing
and longing for a lifetime
of quiet strength.

you came to this place as a cub
and left as a lion,
lifted from angels.

now,
we plant seeds
in your name.

the girl and our gallery

we've made an art out of touching
in perfect darkness. each painting
is on display for the lights
that flash by our windows at night.
i can find the brush strokes
that make her skin a masterpiece
and she signs her name discreetly
on my body, like a tattoo.
and we'll mount our love
where the paint is peeling,
never losing the feeling
of creation.

my hand, on her heart

she will be the world,
forever woven in my breath.

she will be the fresh air
that removes me from fog.

she will be the light
that lives beneath my feet
when i am troubled with shadows.

she will be god-like, wrapped in
fierce skin and illuminated lips.

and we will make love
like it's the first time,
every single time.

and she will come to me unfettered;
the echo of natural calm.

the present presence

people keep saying to live each day
like it's your last,
but i say
live like it's your first.

come out of your mind
like you came out of the womb
and open yourself
to the beauty of
unknowing.

be present in the presence.

the future is now
and you wrote the book.
there is no catalog of worry,
no price plan for prayer,
no index for indecisiveness,
no glossy magazine for glory.

you are here.

you learn how to walk without worry,
when questions wash over you
like memories

before you wake up
to the answers
and realize
you were free all along -

free to just
be and
breathe
instead of
holding your breath
for death
to grab a hold
of your soul
and force you into another
world of unknowing.

people always say to live each day
like it's your last.
why not live like it's your first?

redefine what it means
to be beautiful,
taste wine for the first time
and age gracefully
without collecting dust
on the shelf of
your mind.

dialogue with our ghosts

if we go down
this road again,
i am not getting lost
and our love
won't steer us
in the wrong direction.

instead,
we will dump our baggage
in the backseat
and make new memories
on familiar streets.

you will clutch
the steering wheel
of my heart
and we will depart
for a place where
your skin rests peacefully
beneath my fingertips
and the morning
sleeps softly
on your lips.

your kisses
were the key
that turned me on
and started me
but,
please,
help me understand
why our tank was once empty.

tell me why
our path paved the way
for dead ends.
prove to me
that forever
doesn't break
or bend.

if we go down
this road again,
i will throw every map
out of the window
and feel my way
into the direction
of your body,
the landmark
of your skin.

what is of our experience

even in
caged darkness,
we are
blooming.

before shadows
attempt to
erect demons
on the day,
we are breathing
and burning light.

above the swift,
unflinching weight
of time,
our feet dangle
over the edge
like children
and we are
still learning
how to love.

even in
the sour exile
of death,
our skin is soft
and our souls
sweeten a memory.

even at this moment,
a baby is born
and knows
what it feels like
to be completely
and remarkably
free.

EVEN IN THE SOUR EXILE OF DEATH, OUR SKIN IS

SOFT AND OUR SOULS SWEETEN A MEMORY

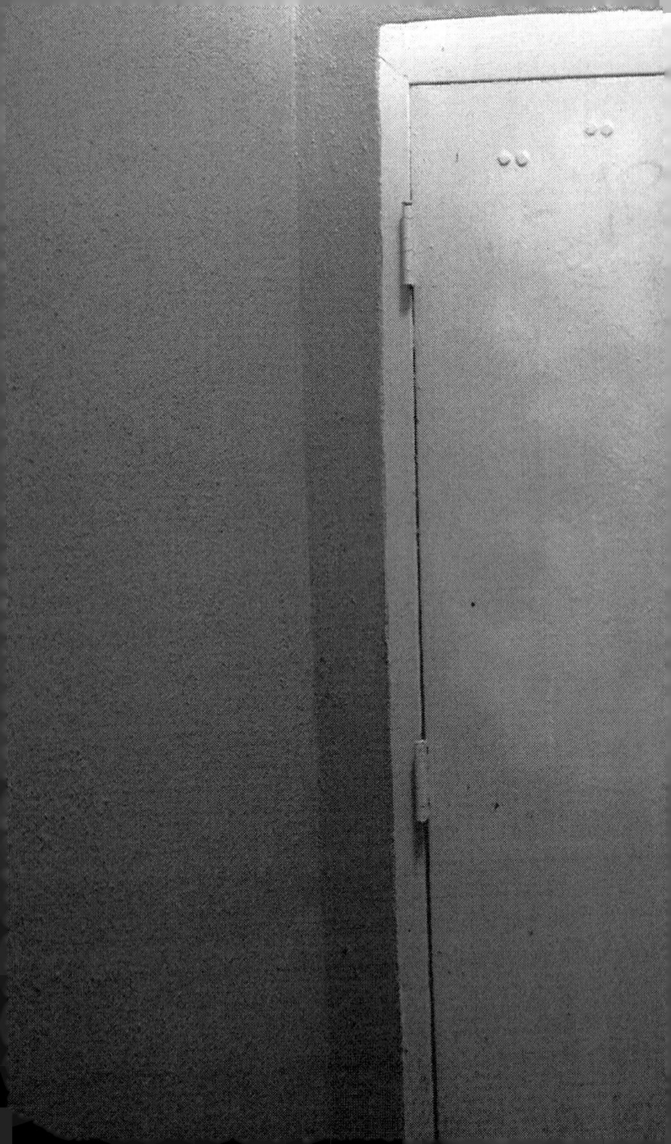

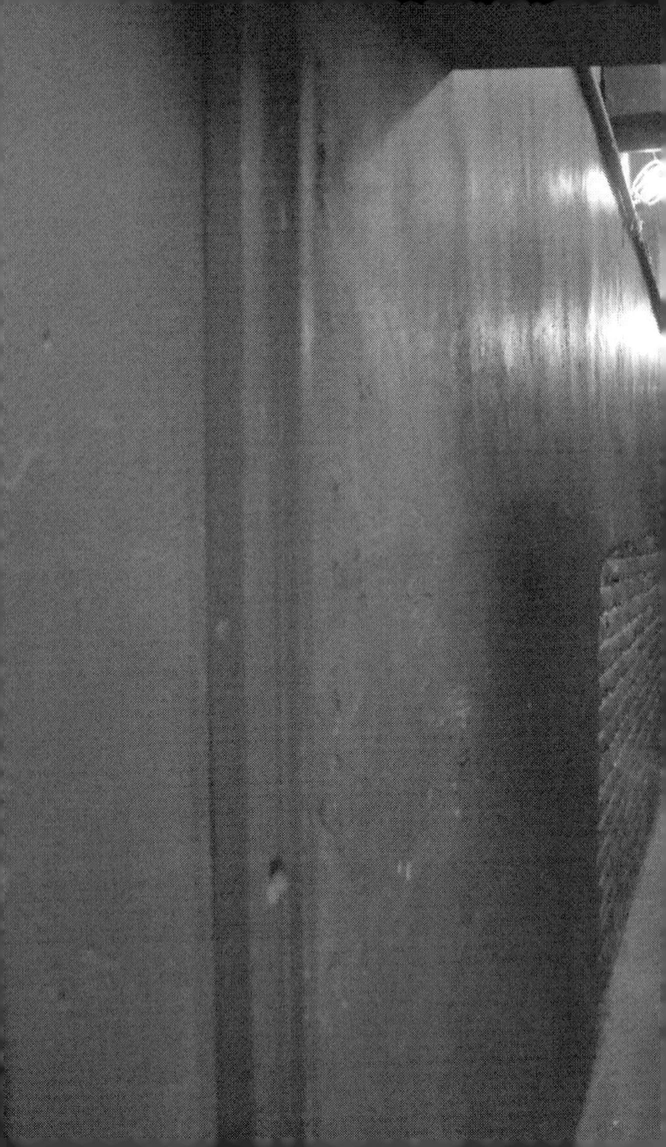

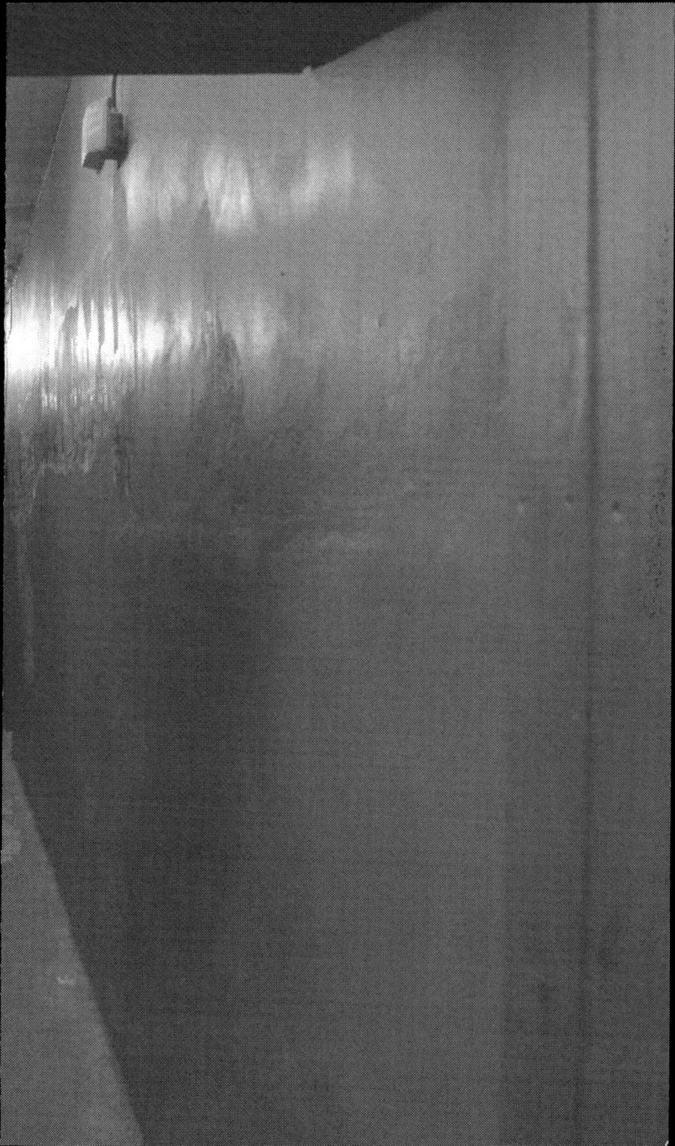

your arrival (an open letter)

love,
if this is the way
hands hold magic,
then i am your servant
and i will seek electricity
in every emotion.

love,
if this is your first impression,
then my heart is too small
and i have wasted too many deaths
in your absence.

love,
if you elude me
for six thousand years
then i am still grateful
for the moments
when you rise like the moon
from behind clouds
and breathe enough light
to ease me into twilight.

love,
if this is my path
then i am unworthy
of your incandescence,
your abundance.

love,
i will one day
make you
my home.

... and she is still dancing

new orleans
is a ballerina
full of dream dust,
dancing in the rain
with her finger
on the pulse of america
and a tattoo
of a broken heart
on her chest.

i fell in love with her
the first time we met.
we held hands
and jumped into
the open arms of color
when she taught me
how to dance.

through clouds of smoke
and singular moments,
i thirst for her tears
and she told me
how death slept
in her bed

and nightmares danced
to the tune of despair.

but new orleans
is wide awake,
splashing puddles of light
on the dry, grey shadows
of her land.

and she is still dancing,
with her finger
on the pulse of america
and a tattoo of a broken heart
on her chest.

the symphony of streetlights

new york is fast approaching madness,
beautifully distant but a bright red
bloodstream, disconnected and
stumbling, splashing puddles of color
on shoestrings, at midnight.
new york is the first step on the way
to forever. an eyeful of wanderlust
singed by fire. drowning in its drinking,
sleeping while standing, at midnight.
new york is sketched on napkins,
a kaleidoscope of silence, bleached out
by the sun. gasping for its gloaming,
a fishbowl of daydreams, swimming
with the streetlights, at midnight.

dewdrops

the seed finds itself in your garden,
planted by the memory of light
beating down on you
and burning your skin
with the blur of desire.

the tides come in with the wind
and you begin to swim,
following your soul's merciless direction -
drowning in kisses dipped in holy water.

and the seed grows inside of you,

twisting and unwinding around your heart
until it holds the key to your rib cage
and you are attracted to the
sunlight that shines
from a fresh set of glowing eyes.

golden

in fifty-one years,
my hands will be
as subtle as time
and as gentle as moonlight
in mid-july.

my fingerprints will
mark moments
without a sense of loss
or any lack of wonder.

in fact,
they will take magic
by the hand
and lead her on a dance
through memories of romance,
of elegantly clutching darkness
during astonishing summers
and slowly unraveling,
then relinquishing,
my ego.

in fifty-one years,
i will sink back into myself
like a child with a new set of eyes
and walk along the streets of brazil,
inching toward perfection,
living in a world
as delicious, and sweet
as honey.

giving birth

do you remember
when the earth was just a baby,
settling in its skin,
safe in the arms of mother nature
with fire breathing from within.
you were not shackled by time
and life roamed around your heart
with the weight of dinosaurs,
leaving footprints in your lungs.
and the first time you saw the sun
you could barely breathe
because the possibility of endless light
planted a seed
so you admire the strength of trees,
who naturally grew into
unwavering beauty,
standing tall,
staring down the mouth of
time.

do you remember
being 11 years old
when your mother told you
"birth is more painful than dying"
and you burst with dreams
without even trying,
seeking light in your heart,
where shadows now rest
comfortably next to fear.
but you come out of the woods clear,
with nature's breath
under your tongue,
and a weightless bliss,
no longer scared of
death.

on the surface and underneath

is our love formless,
like water?

if so,
where do we go
when it overflows
and spills
into our world
like rain?

what happens
when there are
storm clouds
and i slip
into darkness?

do we drink
from the same cup
when there is ice
in our veins
and when we are boiled over,
too hot to touch?

what does water
sound like?

is it the sound
of our kisses
against the rhythm
of the ocean
in the summer?

does it overwhelm us
when we can not swim
and we are broken,
giving birth
to the floods
that lie
deep in our soul?

does water wash over us
like love?

if so,
then what makes us feel dirty
when we are
drowning in intimacy?

and what tides
will push us back
to life?

holding your breath

when there's
an ocean
running through
your house,
you can't
help but
wallow
when the
walls
of your mind
slowly peel
away
like
paint.

suddenly,
you find
yourself
drowning,
searching for
the foundation
of your heart
in the cracks
of floorboards,

as the water rises
and shows you
a reflection
the mirrors
failed to see.

if swimming
is the only option,
you will learn
to fly,
but the
flood lines
remain,
like a stain,
in the
corners of
your home
and the
windows
of your soul.

on meeting/death

walking
steady, he
approaches.

shadow-veiled
and calm,
armed with
the cold breath
of memory,
the tiny storm clouds
of forever.

i am the dawn
of my first footsteps,
the cobalt blue sky
of love,

the stomach-twisting
of my first kiss,

the relentless
stamp
of age.

quietly,
the storms
tumble down
and drown out
the light
of my mind,

until i am
void of misery or

mystery.

it's the ghosts

the stale air wakes her,
thick with memory,
and she recalls his footprints
like a silent language
she can no longer speak.

the morning puts its stamp on the quiet,
when empty shadows lay heavy like death
and whispers of loss
echo through each room.

she once swept away the waves of sorrow,
but dust crept back like the dark
and made a home
in the corner of her mind.

like love, the day is a trespasser -
it's the unwanted fingerprints on mirrors,
the violation of solitude,
the broken glass of the aftermath,
the resurgence of fear.

she checks the locks on each door
walks along the edge of the night,
and heads back to bed.

a resistance

my soul
is hungry,
even though
fruit
falls freely from
the air,
offering branches
of poems
in the warmth
of the sun.

my heart
is light-headed,
even though
a breath
is enough
for nourishment,
and love
is ravenous.

my feet
are tired
of standing
in the circles
of my own maze;
the labyrinth
of my mind.

my clocks
are free,
but they choose
to follow
the same path,
lost
in the redundancy
of time.

the fifth

the first time i died,
i was looking over the edge
of my youth's shadow:
i was a boy,
blackened with road scars
and the troubles of the world
until i traded silence for music
and rode the sound waves
to the shores of adulthood -
feet, still wet.

the second time i died,
i was in my lover's arms:
she was as stable as the wind,
stillborn in my breath
when i was reaching for air.
and the red-haired queen,
blessed with a diamond mind,
awakened me to the absence
of awareness.

the third time i died,
i was a woman:
an earth body,

balancing the pollution of sin
with scars on my skin.
i stood as naked as the trees in november
among the piercing eyes of the cold,
hungry for summer.

the fourth time i died,
i was persephone's son:
a prince drowning in the underworld
of his own mind,
but no longer blind to the site
of my spirit's love affair
with light.

alarm clock (flashing red)

you walked
into me
like
the morning -
sunlight
piercing through
a darkened,
closed mind.

just
as i awoke,
you spoke
and our language
was the language
of the wind,
shaking tree
limbs.

i held
your hand.

unwinding

i
am
so
wound
up
with
songs
that
i
don't
stop
and
listen
to
silence
pull
at
my
heartstrings
and
beg
for
a
dance

NO LONGER BLIND TO THE SITE OF MY SPIRIT'S

LOVE AFFAIR WITH LIGHT

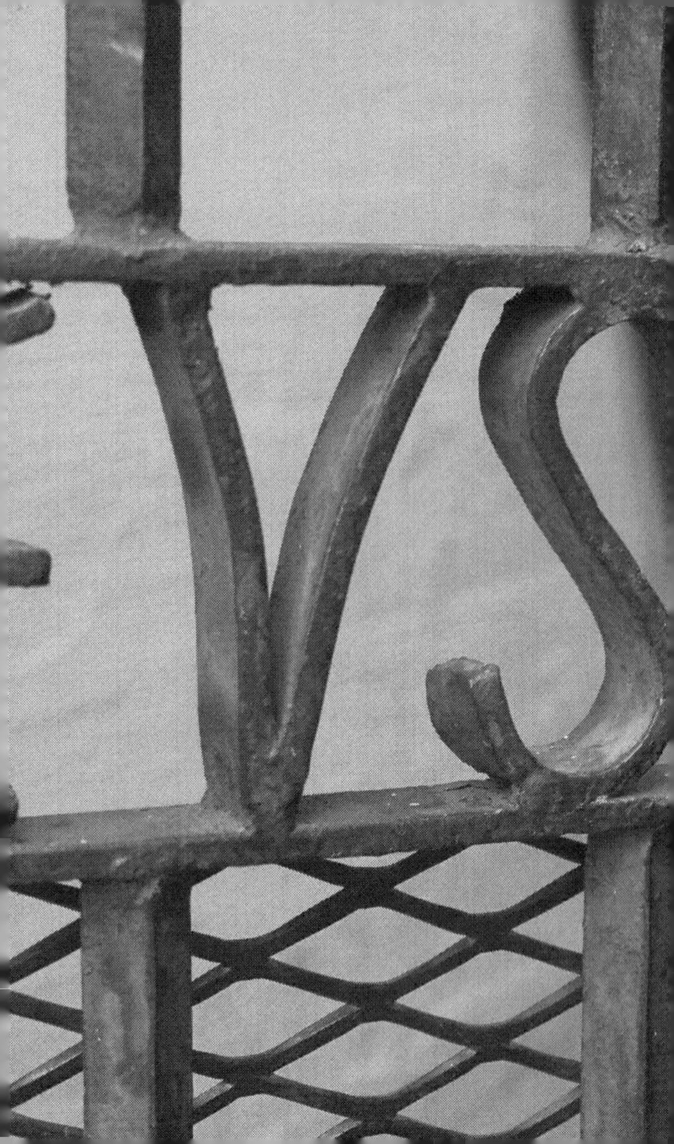

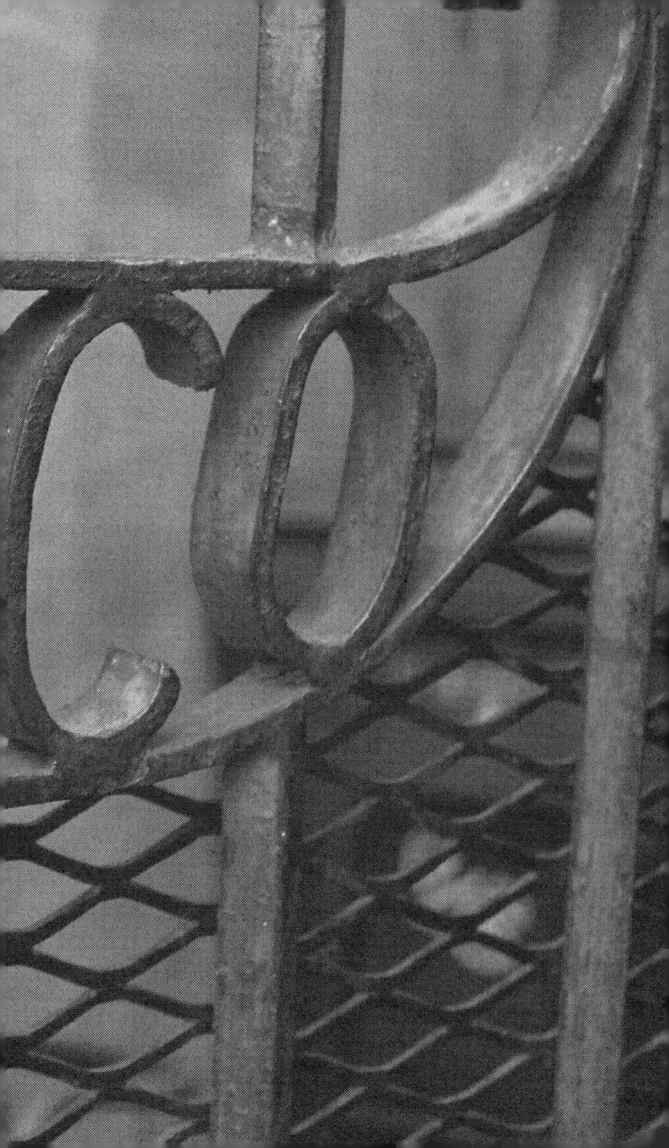

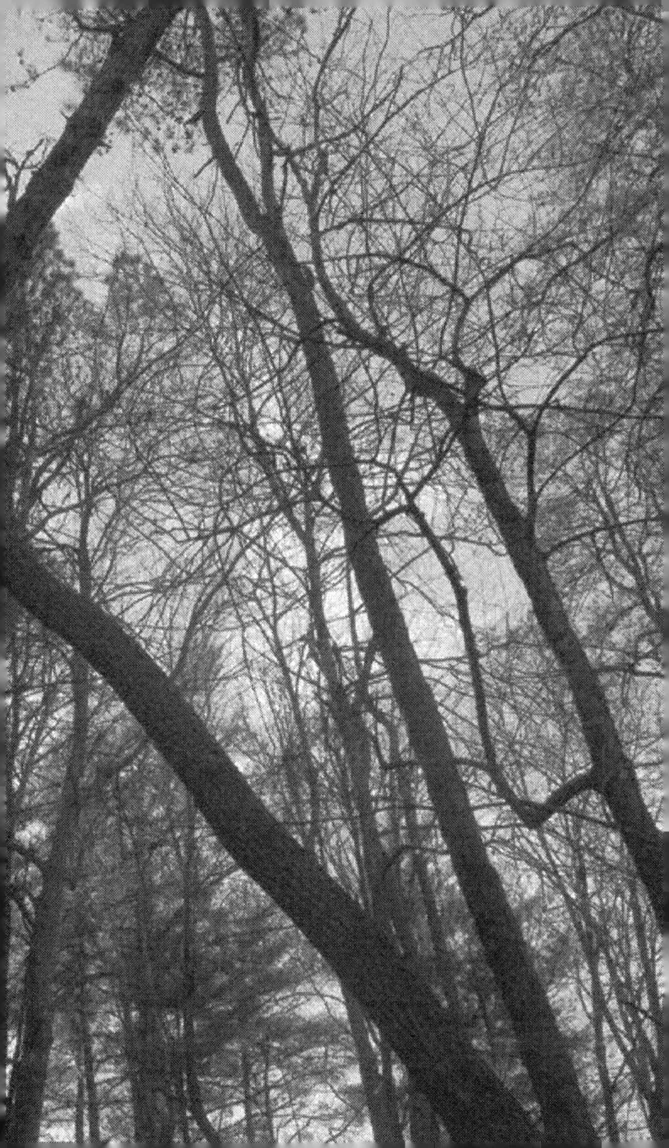

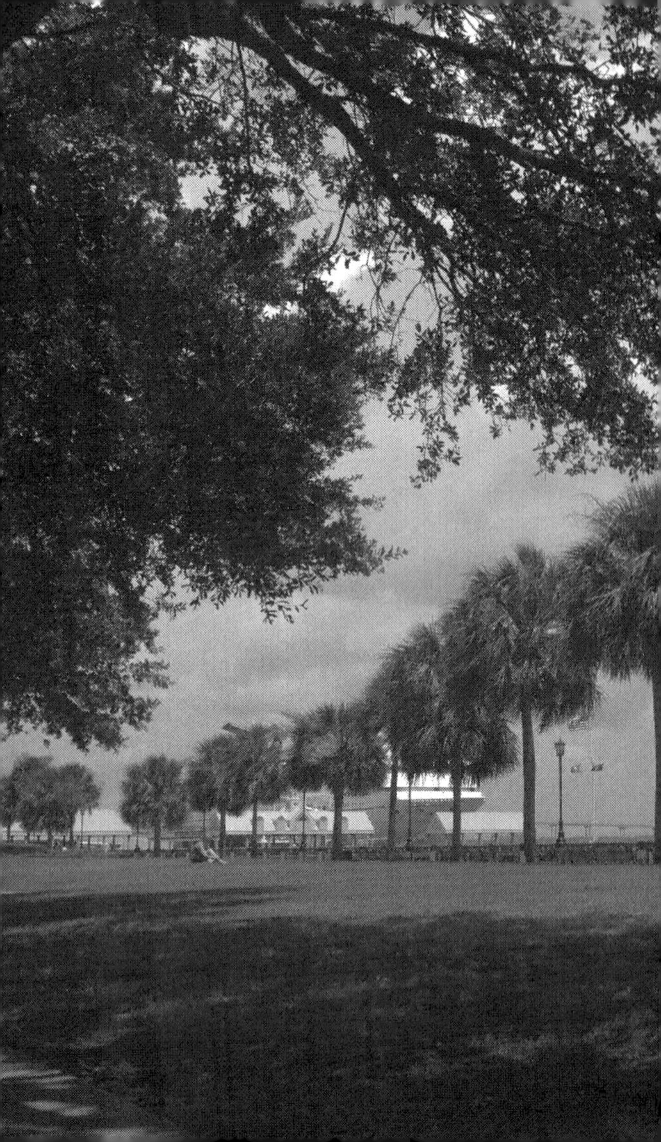

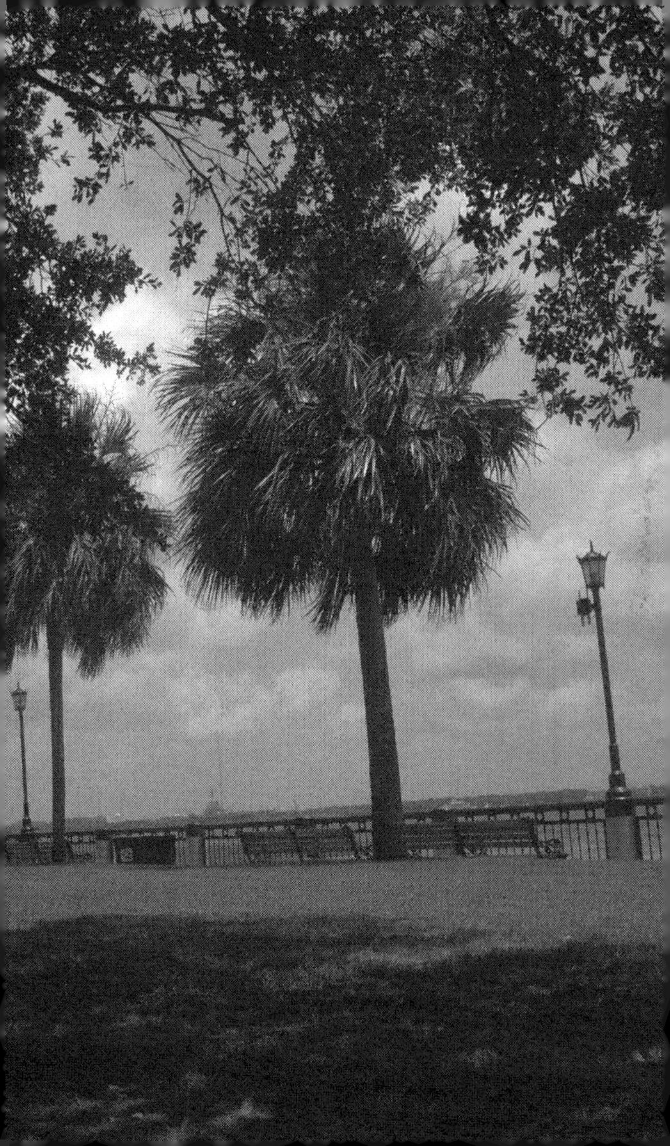

cause justice was not served
on the of
day

four bars = melody
behind bars = prison

melody

one
knows the melody —
its laid out in
a chorus of four bars,
written for the people
who are behind bars,

Kind of melody
its laid out in a
chords of four bars,
for the ~~papanate~~ police
bypassy pasan bars,
sile te copcho

sureness of repetition
~~the~~ melody
laid out in a chords
of

[tenword]

life - pop sings
we are prisoners of
repetition,
and slaves to the rhythm

while looking up

i picked out a cloud and whispered
your name into the wind. a raindrop fell
and i fell into fantasy, moving melodic
above the ground. on a sunny day

i picked out a cloud and felt you
rustle leaves from branches. and thoughts
too light to stand alone blew away
toward the sky. while looking up

i picked out a cloud that scattered
my dreams into the ground. the wind grew
strong and i became weak, letting myself
go to be swept away. on a sunny day.

the tapdancer

your shoes.
they must be tired
of walking back and forth,
here.

i can't help but wonder
how they would move
if you were on stage,

if they had more than just
hallways
to work with,

if this job
allowed music
in the boardroom,

if you saw the
freedom i see
in each
of your
footsteps.

on conversation

she blows a sentence
through my ears and i
dust the letters
out of my head, scrambling to
salvage a familiar sound
through foreign bits
of silence.

we speak in parenthesis,
our language is unnecessary.
a clutter of verbs
in need of an action,
wasting our breath on watered-down
words.

conversation carries like dead weight
and we are both tired.
periods of distance hide
where exclamation points should be.

communication is filtered through
censored sentences, leaving nothing
but question marks and proof
that we have changed.

she blew silence through
my ears and we both

paused.

after taste

she sings like nina simone
and pierces her voice
through a smoky bar
that grabs my ears
as sour candy tickles
the throat of a child
for the first time,
leaving them
wanting more.

i'm tongue-tied
with cosmopolitan kisses
and cherry-red martinis.
she's put a spell on me.

she writes like ani difranco
and tiptoes through the room. i
adapt to her shape and we slide
into each other without speaking.

she bites her lip
to cut through the silence
and i squint at the site
of beauty.

she moves like sade moves
through speakers
and fills up the space
with her after-taste.
i'm drunk with desire,
it's a sweet
taboo.

the lights awaken
and the smoke lingers on my
clothes.

dry

she grows weary of climbing
and tasting her sweat
on someone else's muscles.
her desire is swimming in salty tongues
and fingerprints on flesh,
mounting an illusion
with flashes of matter.

she is wet with words
whispered on napkins
or shouted with graffiti
on abandoned buildings.
pairing her body
with one that is vacant,
hollowed emotion and heavy with echoes.

she knows her ocean is vast and endless
and people spend days
trying to ride her waves
but the sun beats down on her body,
burned
peeling a stranger's skin
off her back.

she rises and finds that sand is everywhere,
slipping beneath sheets
and sliding between toes.
staking a claim like temporary tattoos,
fine reminders of dirty promises
and splashes of another
washed-up dream.

the fabric of us

I.
i grew up with the blood of strong women.
sure of the natural assurance
that flowed quietly
from my grandmother.
she passed it on to me with an elegant whisper,
giving me the message loud and
clear.

II.
it's 8:10 p.m.
and her sister is holding on
to her underlying presence
with the strength of those before her,
looking up at me to remind herself
that my eyes are her eyes,
staring back between generations
and the soft, blinking lights
that remind us she's still
alive.

III.
we are all enlivened with
threaded heartbeats,
weaving whispers from those who have
long since lost their voice.
rely on it, then amplify it
and give it the volume it
deserves.

charlotte and i

are folded into each other and
naked. two pieces of paper, once blank
now full of words we don't speak, we don't
do anything but breathe proximity.
charlotte has poems in her head and i suck
the words out until they are overflowing
on sheets. knowing we don't have to read
between the lines this time. this time we
are nude, not hiding behind metaphors or
synonyms. our limbs are wet with slips of
tongue, her lips are dipped in gold. i kiss
her everywhere with flexible fingers and
map out our story on her body. it glows
on her skin and the plot goes in and out of
context. what's next but sex. tension is tied
up and friction rides up through sound.
we are dirty and divine, stamping each
other with heat inside an envelope of arms.
charlotte is easy to write about. i clutch her
curves and compose a composition,
literally and figuratively. no fantasy this
time. this time we are real, riding the back
of the moon until the sun takes us to
morning.

brushstrokes

from the tip of your hesitance
to the bottom of our cadence,
we are puzzling pieces
scrambling toward each other
to reveal an imperfect pair.

drawn together by the memories
of elusive painters, whose colors
spill over into the way we
look at each other and
speak.

i come to you, weak
with washed-out emotions
and water colors
dripping from my frame.

there are brushstrokes where i bleed
and colors that compliment your
kisses.

come with me
and strip the coat off of our walls
to consider the possibility
of a clearer
picture.

life in layers

no two
poems are
exactly the
same and
no two
songs are
exactly the
same. yet,

despite their
differences, they
somehow manage
to read
along and
sing along
and get

along. each
of us
co-exist among
clashing sunsets
and distant
drumbeats, posing
as one.

and somehow
we manage
to keep
breathing.

a study in stasis

i never knew what silence looked like
until he couldn't speak.
but there it stood,
sitting in the corner of the bedroom
and watching as i
searched for sonic waves
in the thin, gray strands of his hair.

we did everything we could
not to face it.

i remember his boots
waking me up at 3 a.m.
before he went fishing
and nervous laughter
settling in between small talk.

when it finally arrived,
i still tried to ignore it.
but i held his hand
and knew he felt it was coming
all along.

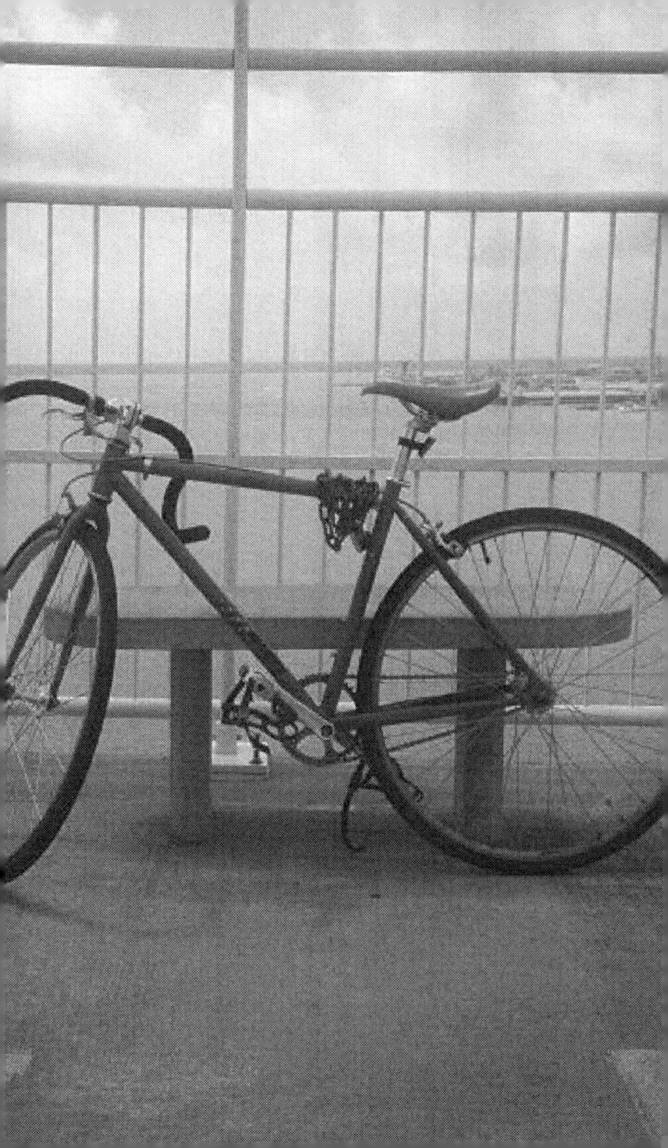

birthmarks

i came away
from our conversation
with your words burned on my skin.
the marks left tattoos
in places where only shadows have been.
in times like these
you overcome by body
and my blood runs a little thicker.

in this corner
lies the secrets of my solitude,
where late-night workout sessions
find inspiration sparing with insomnia.

in that corner,
silence becomes an instrument
for spoken word soundscapes
and my voice
finds the music
that's hiding in notebook paper.

i come away
from our conversations
a little less light-headed,

a little more
naked
than before.
and i notice
people reading poems in my eyes,
trying to make out stories
from the ink on my skin -

they are not scars.

(the blood that runs)

o, love -

this is the sound
between applause, when

dreams reach for
frigid blankets and

wake you up in your
own sweat, with no

breath inside or beside
you, just the smell of

perfume sleeping on
sheets. and you come

in like the dawn, with
the promise of spring's shadow

bursting through the
cracks in the floor. o,

love - will you kiss-clean
the memory of encores and

leave me deaf-blind and hungry
for the taste of this silence, the

taste of this silence.

we speak the same language

our minds are our bodies.
when we lay together,
i shift my thoughts
from words to movement,
searching for a comfortable space
in your silence
to place my hands
along the contours of conversation.

this is sacred.

give me one reason
to fight for hunger
when words are fruit
and your sentences
fit my soul like skin;
when there is substance in patience.

we are lovers of a different kind.
when we sleep together,
sheet music covers our bed
and i dream of songs
that escape me, softly,
in the morning.

your mind moves
like an instrument.
i welcome the chords
willingly.

vertebrae

love rests in your hands like an eagle
who suddenly settled upon
the solitary home of sensitive skin.
she reads your palms
like road maps, tracing the
outlines of history. and her claws
cut to the bone, but you bleed out
the pain and clear your heart
for the promise of flight, the
freedom to let yourself
go.

we found each other chasing the sky,
waiting for stars to form from
the warm, dark air. on our way there,
we caught birds. and they reminded us
that our minds defy gravity,
our lungs embrace the wind,
our bodies know no fear of
falling.

WORDS ARE FRUIT AND YOUR SENTENCES FIT MY

SOUL LIKE SKIN

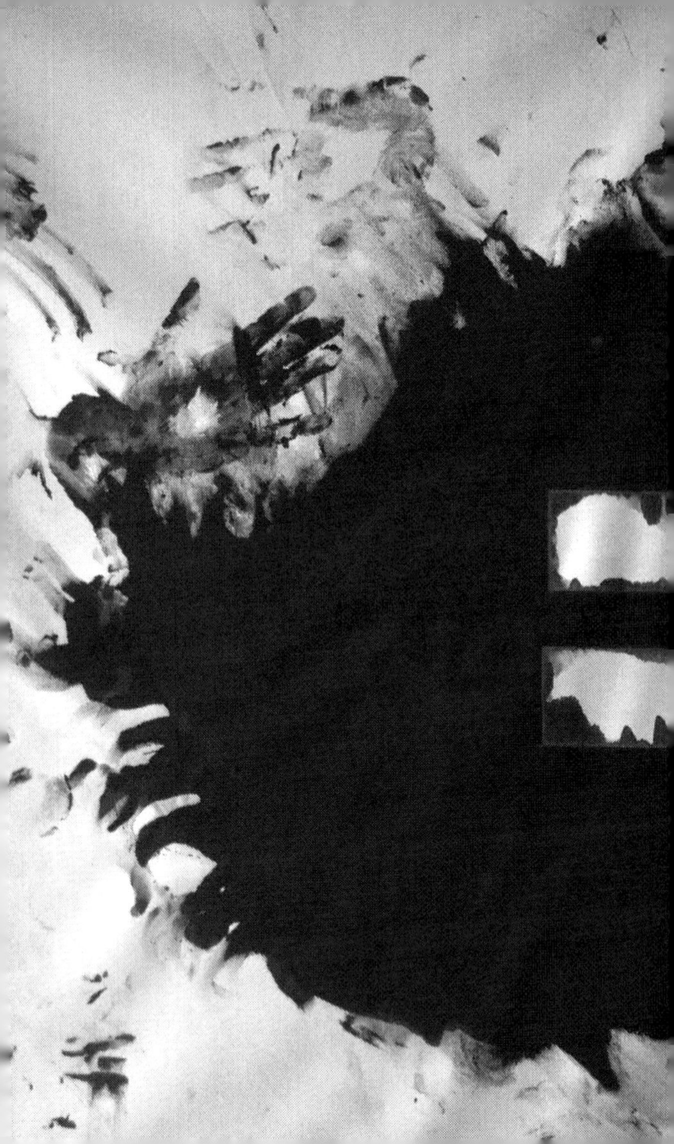

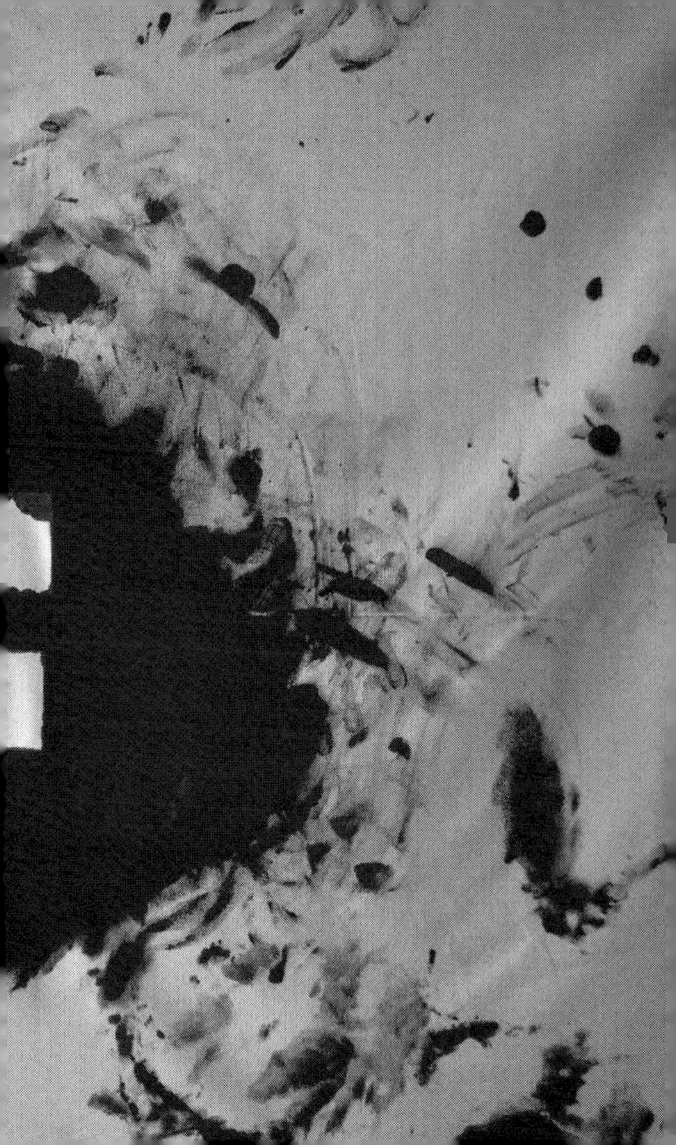

ANIMATION
by TAPE LOOP

ISBN 9781475177772

**CALL ME
BY M
TRUT
BEFOR
YO
CALL
BY
NA**

marcus amaker loves
listening to vinyl and writi
be unse
in charleston, sou
this is hy

WWW.MARCUSAMA

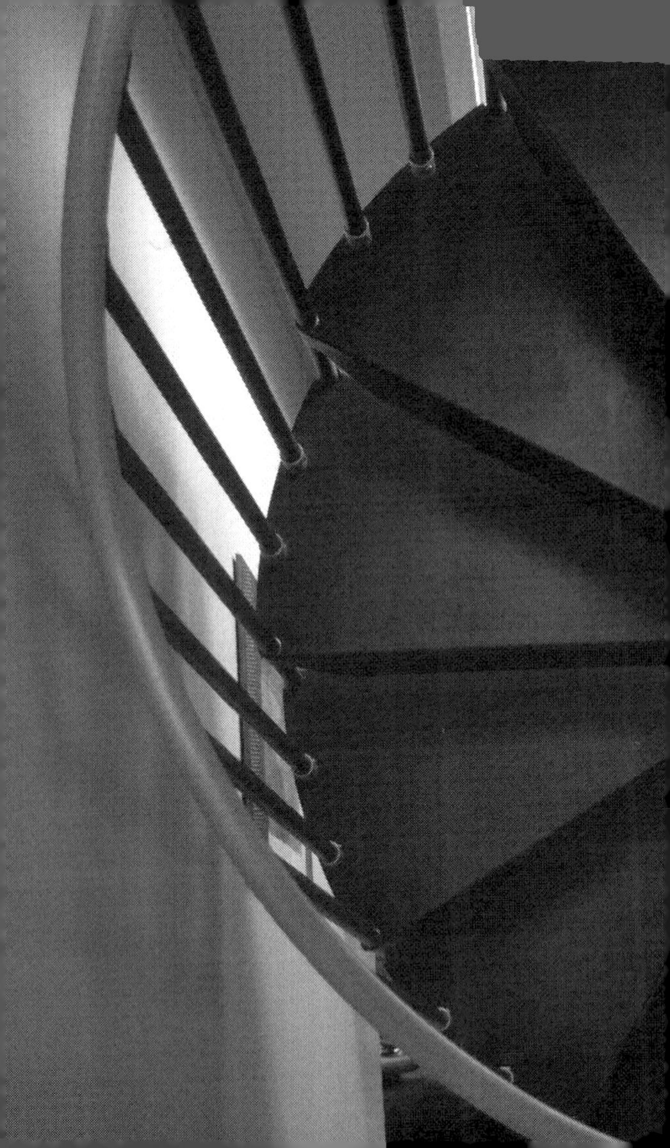

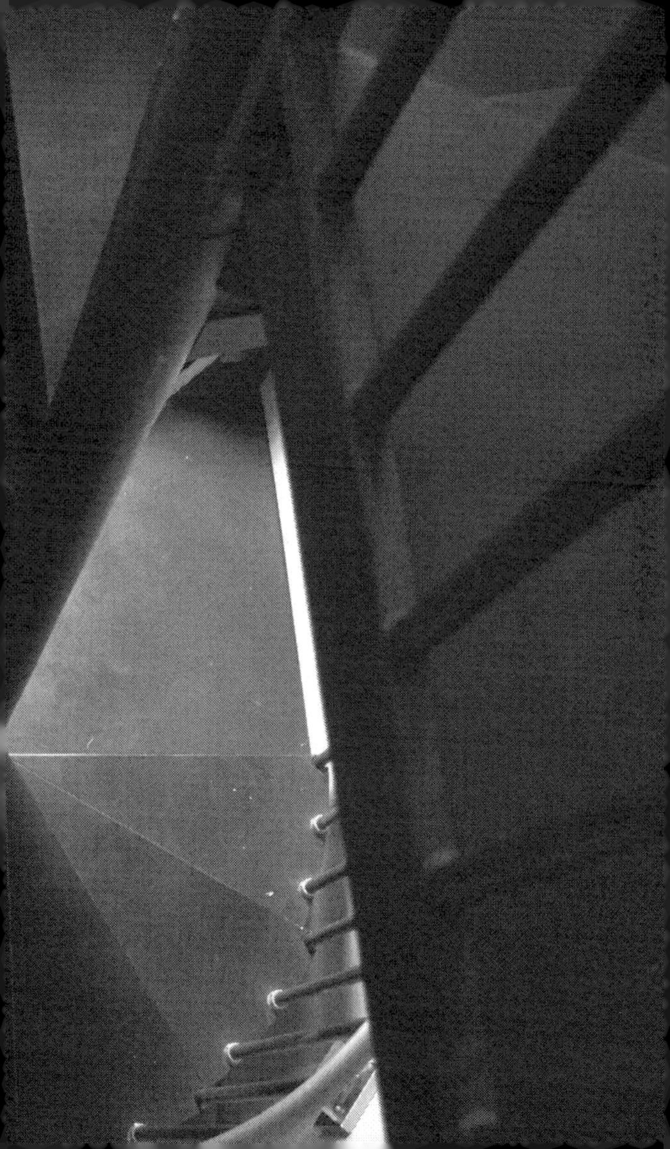

under our dream's illusion

we willingly walked
on an imaginary beach.
our feet,
shuffling through the illusion of fine sand.
our hands
open to the abundance of the ocean,
clutching promises with
dry, cracked skin
as the apparition of water
overflowed with indecision.

we willingly talked
about each other as ghosts.
floating above form,
our skin, once warm,
now cold to the touch
of real love,
buried beneath an imaginary landscape,
a lifetime of delusion.

we willingly bought
into a false story.
each chapter, darker than the last.

our past,
the playwright
of an unfinished scene,
pushing toward
a familiar conclusion.

there are so many things
we can not see.

when her eyes
became black pearls
bathed in shadow,
she still saw
the beauty in us.

each morning,
she awoke
to the crystal clear color
of pure love -
blind to nothing
but our hesitation
to follow.

some people
would rather
crawl through life
and run into the walls
of their mind,

but i'd rather
aim to chase moments

of bliss,
stop to listen
to the whisper
of the wind,
and guide myself
by the endless light inside.

stir the embers

the night unfolds its mystery
through the secret shadows
of our incandescent space.
we are both wearing wings
with borrowed feathers,
clutching the memory of clouds.

tonight, we'll look down
at the ruins of our past
and attempt to rebuild cities
as the wind holds our hand heavenward,
triggering the memory of flight.

on the day we died,
i found pieces of gravity
seeping from the walls,
dissecting the slant of time.
thoughts that once flew
out of the windows
lay grounded in exile,
absorbing the memory of loss.

learning to live wicked

her lipstick licking lollipops leaves me
lusting for the low end of her landscape.
i'd willingly allow her to leak endorphins
into my wounds until my darkened scars
become illuminated and my inhibitions
become emancipated. loneliness, leave
your lack of passion at home as i look
inside of her silence for a lullaby to lull us
into dreams as our arms are locked into
each other and our arms are locked into
the language of sleeps heartbeat. love, this
is lust. this is legs being lifted, this is
learning to live wicked, this is bodies all
twisted and formless like liquid. love, this
is lust.

heartbeat songs

I.
and what is of this life?
oh - open soul, brilliant and burning
with possibility, where beauty is blackened
and black is beautiful. where the laziness of
the afternoon was the only heart beating
in the room and silence sung a song in
perfect pitch. but there goes the clock -
tick-tocking toward enlightenment,
where you can smell the divine lust for
perfection inhaling cigarette-lit dreams.
everything is as it seems. i am the poem
that pieces the peace together, blowing
the dust out of warm pockets that once
held cold bits of reality in the form of
falsehoods from fortune cookies,
now - the frayed edges of love letters.

II.
and what is of the sun? who looks like
God when i close my eyes, whose warmth
has the potential for electric fire, whose
cardinal glow keeps me awake, awake, day-
dreaming, feigning for a song to be woven
into my skin. how did this begin? bright

moon eyes, invincible, piercing and playful, perfectly imperfect and personable. it writes songs and i want to do more than just play along.

III.
and what is of the future?
which poet let go of san francisco?
who let the past slip into fables and fairy tales without happy endings?
who can justify being unjust?
who decided it was cool to look in the mirror and not see lust?
i am in love with tomorrow as i am in love with music - songs that tell stories, whether pregnant with metaphors of unborn children or void of a voice, the melody of my heart.

the cloudbuster

i built
a ladder
to the sun
before
my feet
were ready
for the climb.

there were
blisters
in my heart
and fear
in my breath
but
i walked up
each step,

clutching
the sides of a daydream
with reality's
death grip,
slowly
falling up
to her
warmth.
along the way

i let go
of gravity
and pain
before
finding out
my mind
held on to doubt
like the clouds
hold on to shadows
before
giving birth
to rain.

i built
a ladder
to the sun
before
my soul
was ready
for the climb.
but this time,
ascension is
not distraction
and i
will
not
look
down.

wayfaring (the lost and found)

where wonder ends
and knowing begins,

we shield ourselves
from the glow of uncertainty
and focus on forever.

the road ahead
is not paved in gold,
but we've finally
passed the past,

leaving tire tracks
on the dead ends
of the future
and fire tracks
on the uphill climb
toward each other.

on this journey,
we've strolled along
pathways of rough terrain,
wandering through
detours of broken highways.

on this journey,
i've seen your light
brighten my heaven
and i've watched your darkness
compliment my shadow.

where wonder ends
and knowing begins,

the black does not fall
out of the sky at midnight

and the sun grants us
permanent passage

in the gloaming

I.
if we stop counting time,
it becomes a distant hum
underneath our breath
that never changes tune
and we can live without
giving weight to
the invisible scars
of age.

II.
if life is in the longing,
then i will live forever.
and moments will not be marked
by minutes,
but the number of hairs
that stand up on your arm
when the night dances
like two lovers
unaware of the morning song
of dawn.

au fait

you are
not the stars, lying still
against the fog of dark skies.

not the dream
diverted for distraction,

not the heart
that forgot to pump life
through veins

not a million fragments
of dust dug up from
a perfect annihilation.

you are
the summer of my first memory,

the sun-cloud too high
to touch,

the light
shining shadows on scars.

awakened (part 2)

little boy,
shake yourself awake
from lucid
nightmares,
wipe off the dust
of unrealized daydreams,

bend
when you see
straight lines
and bleed
for
love.

and when your toes
graze the top
of secret graves,
you will live
louder
than the kiss of spring
and steal
sunlight
away
from shadows.

little boy,
this is the beginning
of the beginning,
when you break down
the sound barrier
of
your
own silence
and surf the
top
of sine waves -

do not
be afraid.

we are, lifelines

(one)
take a chance on the river.
push the tide back
when you get here
and clear the way
for the water's reflection.
there's so much to see
when you look down
with the sun as your wallpaper
and clouds in the background.
be jealous of the red
that colors your hair,
then outline the footsteps
that got you there
and don't be afraid
to call yourself beautiful.

(two)
they say scent keeps its grip on memory
i hear that we keep forgetting
our senses, throwing dead sentences
out to sea.
can you see me
swimming through sunken thoughts
and sliding through unscented kisses

waiting for solitude to free its stench
from my shore.

(three)
rain clouds have come down on you
and i shield what i can
with my hand reaching out for yours.
tonight, let your tears
tell me what your voice can not.
tonight, i will lay with you
in a pool of memory
and be there when you come up for air.

mantra

never get attached to
someone who's detached from
choices that make sense and
a thirst that can't be quenched, for
tires that wear thin on
a road to a dead end and
bumpy rides through dirt. they
have a willingness to hurt the
people in their path who
guide them from the crash, but
what's a slower speed when
thrill is what they need, so
never get attached to
someone who's detached from
choices that make sense.

star

i'll stop for you.
        park my car
        on some abandonded
road and look up.
don't be afraid to
        come down
and fall next to me
        so we can abandon
our fear
for this night.
then walk down
an empty street
        and drain the sky
of its clouds
until each star is clear.
let's abandon
our obsession with gravity
        and release it
to the sky
until
you have to return
        and leave my hands
immaculate and brilliant,
burning with
stardust.

EVERY MOMENT THAT YOU ARE ALIVE

IS THE ONLY MOMENT THAT MATTERS.

CLIENTS

INCANDESCENCE

INCAN

INCANDESCENCE.

glass ceilings
crashing down
floats inside
of expectation
tiptoed around

walking on
broken pieces of light
swept under the rug
this morning, the light
broke through my mind's shadows —
it looked like a woman —
the sun was not

love

i cut off all of my strings
now i'm not hung up on things.

i dusted off my wings
so i wouldn't cling to things.

and i started to fly -

free of gravity -
to tiptoe through the wind,
rid myself of sin
and learn to live again.

and love gave me a pen,
and told me to write about my freedom.

hate was rattling my cage
and i refused to feed him,

because
truly letting myself go
means living out loud
and cradling the clouds

and suddenly

my space sucked its deep black holes
back into oblivion.

my affinity for flight
unearthed a new kind of light

and love guides me through the night,

she says, "keep me in your sight."

i do
and she opened me up

to you.

side effecting

close my eyes
to welcome the dark
and squint to adjust
to the light inside.

i stumble across
an unswept floor,
reaching for something
or someone
stable.

breaking mirrors
along the way
and lights illuminating
the scars of time.
tangled between
a telephone chord,
searching for something
stable.

a window retreats
into its sadness
within the reach
of troubled hands

and with a new light
I'll open my eyes,
looking for something
stable

carolina

every time i tell myself
i'll stop writing about her,
i start writing about her
and the way she dances.

you see,
she dances as if dancing
were the only way to move
and i'm plugged in
to her groove.

i'm wired into my desire
for her sonic boom
because we are in tune.

and on the days we dance together,
our footsteps shuffle through the streets,
gracefully.

arm in arm,
she leads me into poetry
and we rely on each other
rhythmically and spiritually.

but when she lets go,

i unsuccessfully search for the same sound
elsewhere.

faking music with off-key melodies
and turning up the volume
on stagnant symphonies.

but
every time i tell myself
i'll stop wanting her
i start wanting her.

and the rhythm of my heartbeat
is the rhythm of her heartbeat.

and we'll close our eyes
and listen.

the dance

I
the road lays out before me
and i press my ear to the ground
to feel its pulse.

driving on tired wheels
and losing myself
in the beat
of cars dancing around me.

the movement of hours,
like songs
draw me closer
to the start of another story.

II.
again,
the road calls my name.
i answer to find
that nothing has changed
but faces and friends
scattered and stirring
in their own little worlds,

but the music is static
within these walls
so i dance alone
to the rhythm of home.

82 days

she begged them for a gun
when the sun came
when the mundane
days of captivity
gave way to death's gravity.

she no longer flies
but she tries
to hold on to her wings
as solitude
plucks each feather.

she's never
thought about dying before
or trying to score
a plea bargain for her life
but they offer her a knife
and she begs them for a gun.

there's nowhere to run
when the ground's been spun
out from beneath you

when your last breath
will be broadcast

for some newscaster's
solumn tone

somewhere back home
your fairy tale's already being written
typed out and immortalized

for the eyes of mere mortals
who don't know what it's like
to win a staring contest
with
death.

self-portrait (the spark)

as a spoken word poet, i saunter off on sundays to scream from a soapbox on the sidewalks. stanzas scribbled out on sandpaper are smoothed out for the stage. i stitch thoughts together then slide between the sheets as i sleep. it becomes my second skin and i stick metaphors in my pen for self-gratification, it's better than sex. ... and more colorful than saturday morning cartoons. i spit like i'm superman - swooping through the words and fighting off the verbs i've scratched out on small pieces of paper. it obsesses me and undresses me from normal conversation so i sit naked in a sea of ink stains then swim through an endless stream of inspiration, searching for the spark that will help me start the process over again.

patchwork

the threads unravel
and pull away, slowly.
years of working with needles
and nothing to show
but permanent stains
on half-sewn sheets.

there's a closet full
of failed attempts;
of loose-fitting jeans
with holes in the knees
and skin-tight sweaters
hung out of my reach.

i rest under layers
of dirty clothes,
coming apart
at the seams.

rites of passage

yellow and blue stains
define America's roads
where highway signs once lived,

overlooking the landscape's progression
into womanhood.

we once rested comfortably
in mother nature's bosom
before our seeds planted
a different kind of green,
growing across state lines.

America,
why do you live *between* civilization?
silently resting in the dead space
beside rising gas prices
and odd-numbered exit signs

do you grieve for the way it used to be?

when your spirit passed
through open windows
and the blues
slipped beneath backdoors

into the ears of eager speakers
who replayed your music
through word of mouth?

America,
i've watched you make love with the devil
and sell your soul
to the next highest bidder.

i've seen your children
clamor for their mother
during 5 o'clock traffic jams
while listening to the
reconstructed echo of rock stations.

i've come upon
your remains in the dirt
after digging for silence
on overcrowded streets.

But America,
i found you
in the foggy green hills
of West Virginia,
in the dirty drunk streets
of South Carolina,
still beautiful
as ever.

terrorism

black smoke billowed from
burning buildings
and the lazy eye of the morning
begged for another hour
of sleep.

but no alarm clock
can wake us up from this.

from a falling body
trying to miss
the ground.

quick,
tell me why you insist on feeling unlucky.

and while you're at it,
tell me what it's like
to be fucked by gravity,

stuck
thirty thousand miles in the air
with your cell phone
on speed dial,

dialing 911
and no one's home.

long after the call
goes through,
they will use you

to justify four-plus years
of rushing war's fears
down our throats.

it's a hard pill to swallow,
but yet we follow

our president,

the government,

and the little bouncing ball spelling

t - e - r - r - o - r - i - s - m

sunspots

she balances wonder
with a loss of inhibition
and traps sunlight
between each strand of hair

she moves through life's marathon
one sunray at a time
and catches her breath
under the shadows
of endless
possibility

i like spending time there.

resting with her,
not counting the miles
of everyday life
or worrying about a finish line.

time doesn't exist here.

it waits until
we wake up,
covered in golden threads
with traces of sunspots

on my pillows.

i wonder if she noticed me
squinting in the dark
cuddled up to bright,
delicious dreams.

i liked spending time there.

purple heart

the last time i saw you
you were a shadow of yourself -
hiding the battle scars
after declaring war
on the ghosts that were
moving through your body.

we all would have
gone on the front lines for you
but you had to do it alone.
so you held on to your heartbeat
like a weapon -
smiling through the pain
even after your enemy claimed its name:

cancer.

a year and a half later,
your ex-boyfriend tells me
it's a shame that someone
with so much life
couldn't win the fight.
so we drink and think of you
and continue to train for the battle
like it's the only thing to fight for.

and now i sharpen my sword
for your memory
and cut through the silence
that left you here
after all of the smoke cleared.

the summer of our first memory

we are simply the early morning sky, overwhelmed with dreams. the red tongue of a child after succumbing to the sweet sin of strawberries. the familiar smell of old books, haggard and dusty after history latched on to every word. we are the spirit of youth, bursting at the seams. the song that sticks to memory like honey. a blank page, painted with the colors of poems. the train that traces our country's landscape. the feet that dance along patton ave. we are the feeling that skirts along the tiny hairs of your chest when you are mesmerized with love.

the overflow

feelings left unattended
fall like leaky faucets
drip,
drip,
dripping
until you come home
and find your heart
overflowing with
weeks,
weeks,
weekends
of wasting time,
soaking in the shadows.

you can spend
your whole life
watch,
watch
watching
memories float by mirrors
or you can
turn off the waterfall by
tight,
tight,
tightening
the grip on madness,
cleaning up the mess.

WE ARE THE SPIRIT OF YOUTH,

BURSTING AT THE SEAMS.

DEAR CHARLESTON,

photo by jason layne

I LOVE YOU.

POETRY BOOKS
Listening to Static (2005)
Poems for Augustine (2005)
The Soft Paper Cut (2007)
The Present Presence (2012)
Mantra (2015)

available on amazon.com +
marcusamaker.com

ALBUMS
Minimalism (2005)
Dealate (2005)
Escapism (2006)
1945 (2008)
Lady Phoenix (2009)
Digital Detox (2009)
Compilation: Songs Recorded as a Kid (2009)
Sunday Rain (2011)
The Cassette Demos (2011)
Animation (2012)
The New Foundation (with Quentin E. Baxter) (2014)
the drum machine, part 1 (2015)

photo by jordan freeman

work in progress.1

About Bike rides

You've been down this road before,
lacing up your solitude,
tightening down your shoelaces
tight
for the ride.

did the you remember doing this before,
wondering if we out of colors
staring at you, got puzzled
You rose up gracefully
at the road.

Made in the USA
Columbia, SC
08 November 2023